This book is dedicated to all who find Nature not an adversary to conquer and destroy, but a storehouse of infinite knowledge and experience linking man to all things past and present. They know conserving the natural environment is essential to our future well-being.

GRAND CANYON
THE STORY BEHIND THE SCENERY®
by Merrill D. Beal

Merrill (Dave) Beal is a career employee of the National Park Service and has been active since 1943 in protecting and interpreting our natural wonders and historic places. He is well acquainted with Grand Canyon National Park, having served there as chief park naturalist for many years. A graduate of Idaho State University and Utah State University, with major studies in zoology and resources management, Dave has a broad natural-history background and is known and respected for his work in this field. He is now the regional director for the Midwest Region of the National Park Service.

Cover: Grand Canyon sunset; photo by Ray Atkeson. Inside cover: Mount Hayden, North Rim; photo by David Muench. Title page: Kaibab squirrel; photo by Dave Beal.

Edited by Gweneth DenDooven; Book Design by K. C. DenDooven
1978 Revised Edition
GRAND CANYON — THE STORY BEHIND THE SCENERY. PUBLISHED BY KC PUBLICATIONS, P.O. BOX 14883, LAS VEGAS, NEVADA 89114. © 1978 KC PUBLICATIONS. L. C. NO. 75-14775. ISBN: 0-916122-06-9 PAPER, 0-96122-31-X CLOTH

The Grand Canyon is an awesome spectacle of nature's grandeur, a classic example of erosion unequaled anywhere on earth. The multi-hued cliffs and slopes of the tremendous chasm descend in a timeless panorama, culminating unbelievably in the dark and somber cleft a mile below, where the Colorado River continues to carve deeper and deeper into the earth's crust

The Grand Canyon demands more than visual inspection. It challenges man's imagination and poses questions which must not go unanswered. How big is it? How was it formed? What discoveries about our planet's history have been made here, where so many layers of the earth's crust are exposed to view?

Knowledge of an area is assembled gradually by the efforts of many observers. It is through the discoveries of others that we enlarge our own knowledge of a subject. First the facts must be uncovered; later they can be correlated and interpreted.

Man's approaches to understanding Grand Canyon are quite varied. Indian legends attribute deep religious significance to the region. Split-twig figurines found deep inside caves in the canyon walls provide physical evidence of prehistoric man's use of the canyon about 4,000 years ago.

Modern man may also find a spiritual or philosophical awakening at Grand Canyon. In gaining an understanding of nature's works, man can better understand himself. Through the physical challenge of hiking canyon trails or the mental discipline of understanding constant change, destruction, and creation, many visitors experience not only recreation but *re-creation*, and their lives are greatly enriched.

For some people the need for self-expression—the wish to communicate feelings to others—becomes a driving force. Grand Canyon has inspired great poetry and prose, outstanding works of art, and magnificent music. This one subject brings forth a wide variety of forms and meanings from different artists.

Scientists, too, have found the canyon a great challenge. While science is really little more than man's organized effort to understand nature's laws, the path of progress from observed fact into the unknown is strewn with many obstacles. Carefully developed and nurtured theories are cast aside as new facts emerge.

For more than a century, learned men have studied the Colorado River and its grandest canyon. They have pieced together an amazing story of earth-building and erosion that spans the last two billion years of earth's history. But scientific theories must often rely upon relative likelihood rather than positive evidence. Studies still go on. The Grand Canyon story is subject to constant revision as knowledge increases.

Preceding page: The Colorado, river through time; photo by Ray Atkeson

JOSEF MUENCH

The Grand Canyon is nature's finest monument to the combined forces of uplift and erosion aided by an unlimited amount of time. Obviously the chasm was carved from the same solid rocks which now form its walls. Most of the work was done by the Colorado River and its tributaries, but the process has been very gradual. Nature works more slowly than man in most instances. (When she works rapidly, we view the results as catastrophic and resent their effects upon the puny efforts of men.) History

The Canyon

shows us that man's works endure best where he has learned to live in reasonable harmony with the natural environment.

The changes which man has brought about on the face of the land are obvious. Each of us can remember a time when an area now covered with homes was farmland. We can also recall changes in roads, development of reservoirs, canals, and other modifications to our environment. But, in our memories, the land itself—plateaus, rivers, canyons, and mountains—has always been as it is now. In terms of a single human lifetime, this may be true; but studies of the physical evidence reveal interesting stories about changing land forms everywhere in the world.

The Colorado River has performed its greatest work in northern Arizona. Here earth sculpture reaches its grandest proportions. The river turns from its southerly course through sixty-two miles of the Marble Gorge and plunges westward through the Kaibab Plateau, imprisoned in a narrow gorge a mile below the canyon rims. (*Kaibab* is a Paiute Indian word meaning "mountain lying down.") Historically this portion of the river's course, from the mouth of the Little Colorado River to the Grand Wash Cliffs, was called Grand Canyon. It measures 217 river miles in length. Today the entire distance from Lees Ferry above Marble Canyon to the Grand Wash Cliffs is called Grand Canyon—a distance of 277 river miles!

The spectacular central portion of the canyon averages about nine miles in width from rim to rim, but in places promontories are as little as four miles apart. The greatest width, eighteen miles, is measured between embayments. In contrast, the width at the eastern end in Marble Canyon is as little as a tenth of a mile. Viewing distance from the South Rim to the river averages about three miles, but from the North Rim the distance is twice as great.

The canyon floor is about 4,500 feet below Grand Canyon Village and 5,700 feet below Bright Angel Point on the North Rim. Thus the round figure of one mile usually offered as the depth measurement of the canyon is reasonably accurate.

THE COLORADO—CARVER OF CANYONS

A mighty river capable of such earth sculpture must start somewhere. The Colorado rises high in the Colorado Rockies in Rocky Mountain National Park. The distance from the source across the high-plateau country and down to the Gulf of California measures 1,450 miles.

A major contributor to the torrent is the Green River, which begins in the Wind River Mountains of Wyoming and travels 720 miles through canyons and parks to join the Colorado in Canyonlands National Park, some 1,100 miles above its entry to the gulf. The Colorado and its tributaries drain a land area of over 240,000 square miles. There are many canyons along the river's course, and the stream drops 10,000 feet over hundreds of rapids in its descent from the mountains to the sea.

The river has been given many names in a variety of tongues. The Spaniards called it the *Rio Colorado* (Red River), and Americans adopted an English translation, "Colorado River." The name was appropriate, for the river was indeed red (or brown), due to the color of the sand and mud carried with the current. The wild, turbulent Colorado ran untamed for centuries. Its surging waters moved along at speeds ranging from two and one-half to twelve miles per hour, where measured near Bright Angel Creek, and its depth varied from ten to eighty feet or more. (The average velocity of the

From the North Rim at Toroweap Point, the rock sheers away in a dizzying descent to the ancient ribbon in time that is the Colorado River.

White-capped waves attest to the power of the Colorado's current.

K. C. DEN DOOVEN

river at present is 4.2 miles per hour, but through the rapids the mean velocity is 7.5 to ten miles per hour.)

Accurate records maintained by the United States Geological Survey gauging station in the bottom of Grand Canyon show that the volume of flow of the river has varied from a trickle of 700 cubic feet per second on December 28, 1924, to a measured flood of 127,000 cubic feet per second on July 2, 1927. Upstream from Grand Canyon, high-water marks left by a flood which took place July 8, 1884, were used to compute a maximum flow of 300,000 cubic feet per second!

The ability of a stream to move materials increases much more than in the direct ratio to its volume. Thus, a river does its greatest work of transportation during flood stages. The load of suspended solids and dissolved material carried by the Colorado River has varied from a few hundred

The elegant forms of fluted rock grace a pocket which serves as a haven for boatmen and a respite from the challenge of the river's dynamic force.

The swirling currents of a silt-laden Colorado River have polished by abrasion the hard schist and granite of the Inner Gorge and sculpted it into forms of delicate beauty. Such river-water sculpture is called "stream fluting."

BILL BELKNAP

tons a day at low water to a maximum of 27,600,000 tons per day during a flood on September 13, 1927. The average load per day over a span of many years was 391,780 tons.

The following example illustrates what a tremendous feat was thus accomplished by the river: If only the approximate 400,000-ton *average* burden were loaded into dump trucks of five tons capacity each, it would take 80,000 trucks going by at a rate of less than a second apart for twenty-four hours just to do the same amount of work the river did quite naturally each day.

In addition to the transporting of suspended and dissolved materials, the river also moved a large load of pebbles and boulders—by rolling or bouncing them along the bottom of its channel. The amount of this load has not been accurately determined, but it may have almost equaled the amount of suspended solids.

These were the materials which aided the Colorado River in its slow but inexorable wearing away of layer after layer of rock to create the fantastic landscape we know. All of the debris came from somewhere upstream, and it was going somewhere downstream. Rates of erosion have varied from place to place, but studies show that the overall rate of denudation for the entire Colorado River drainage area has been six and one-half inches or more for each 1,000 years.

The Colorado and its tributaries gather the products of erosion in all the inaccessible reaches of the plateau country and transport them to new localities. They once came to rest at the mouth of the Colorado River where it empties into the Gulf of California. Over a long period of time, sediments built up a vast delta here and also filled in the Imperial Valley.

Hoover Dam, on the Colorado River below Grand Canyon, was completed in the mid-1930s, backing up the large body of water that is now Lake Mead. In that area the Colorado was subdued at last. But from the geologist's point of view, lakes—including those made by man—are only temporary features. As soon as they start to fill with water, their destruction begins; the sand and silt that once passed through are now deposited in the bottom of the lake. Lake Mead will eventually be filled with sediments. A reasonable estimate of the useful life of the lake is several hundred years.

To further utilize the river and prolong the life

The downward-cutting Colorado River, horizontal rock layers of varying resistance to erosion, and an arid climate have combined to produce a landscape of alternating cliffs and slopes forming stepped canyon walls.

of Lake Mead, a large dam was constructed in Glen Canyon, upstream from the Grand Canyon. The gates of Glen Canyon Dam were closed in 1963, and a new lake was formed—Lake Powell, named for Major John Wesley Powell, an early explorer of the area.

Lake Powell now absorbs about four-fifths of the sediments carried by the river, and its existence will probably triple or quadruple the lifetime of Lake Mead. Clear water is released from Glen Canyon Dam, and a controlled Colorado flows onward through Grand Canyon. It is often green in color, but at times it regains a measure of its former muddy appearance when tributary streams (such as the Paria or Little Colorado rivers) flood. The load of sediment measured now averages about 80,000 tons per day, about one-fifth as much as the river carried when it ran wild and unchecked.

So the Colorado has temporarily lost its power to move tremendous quantities of sand and boulders; it now obeys man's commands. But Grand Canyon remains as a dramatic tribute to the power of that river, a power that cannot be fully comprehended by any man.

SUGGESTED READING

DELLENBAUGH, FREDERICK S. *The Romance of The Colorado River*, Chicago: The Rio Grande Press, 1962.

MATTHES, FRANCOIS E. "The Grand Canyon of the Colorado River." *Bright Angel Quadrangle Topographic Map.* Washington, D.C.: United States Department of Interior Geological Survey, 1962.

MORTENSEN, A. R. "The Colorado . . . River of the West." *Utah Historical Quarterly*, Vol. 28, No. 3. Salt Lake City: Utah State Historical Society, July, 1960.

SCHUMM, S. A., AND CHORLEY, R. J. "Talus Weathering and Scarp Recession in the Colorado Plateaus." *Annals of Geomorphology*, Vol. 10, No. 1, 1966.

SHELTON, JOHN S. *Geology Illustrated.* San Francisco: W. H. Freeman and Company, 1966.

THROUGH THE EYES OF THE EXPLORERS

The people who lived here in ancient times left no record of their thoughts about Grand Canyon, but the lore of more recent inhabitants has been preserved. Indian legends concerning the origin of the abyss are revealing. They support the oft-made observation that human beings have always felt compelled to provide an explanation for everything they encounter so that they do not suffer discomfort by the existence of such things, however awesome they may be.

The Navajo tell of a great flood brought on by incessant rains. During this time the land was flooded to great depths. Their ancestors were threatened with drowning. But finally an outlet was formed by the rushing waters, and the Navajo survived by being transformed temporarily into fish. The outlet formed by those floodwaters is said to be the Grand Canyon. In deference to their deliverers, some Navajo still refrain from eating fish.

Spanish conquistadores reached the South Rim of Grand Canyon in 1540, guided by Hopi Indians. These first European visitors were members of Coronado's expedition under the leadership of Don Lopez de Cardenas. The conquistadores were mightily impressed by the awesome terrain—even more when three members of the party failed in an attempt on foot to reach the great river they saw far below.

History does not record the thoughts of these

The rising sun sheathes a distant canyon wall in golden color and illuminates the serpentine curves of the timeless Colorado.

men concerning how Grand Canyon was formed. Perhaps the singleness of purpose the Spaniards displayed in their search for gold precluded such speculation.

Spanish missionary priests visited the Grand Canyon region in 1776, and American fur traders followed a half-century later. Again, their objectives may have caused them to view the canyon and surrounding deserts primarily as obstacles to their success.

The first comprehensive report on the Grand Canyon country resulted from the work of a War Department expedition of 1857–58 headed by Lieutenant Joseph C. Ives. His mission was to ascend and explore the Colorado River and to report on its navigability.

Dr. John Strong Newberry was geologist to this expedition, and as they explored the region his practiced eye noted many details, evidence upon which an early scientific explanation and description of the Grand Canyon region would be based. He described its physical features, rocks, and fossils and stated that the canyons of the Colorado had been eroded by the river itself. He wrote:

Having this question [of origin] constantly in mind, and examining with all possible care the structure of the great cañons which we entered, I everywhere found evidence of the exclusive action of water in

"Vasey's Paradise" in Marble Canyon is a notable example of what happens when water percolating through porous rock reaches a layer impervious to its assault: Underground watercourses thus created are liberated through the walls of the canyon, tumbling forth through cascades of greenery to join the river. Major Powell, the first to descend the river, named this lush oasis for his eastern botanist friend, Vasey.

Eons of time and countless tons of water, sand, and silt have polished the marble in Marble Canyon to a degree that any sculptor on earth would envy.

their formation. The opposite sides of the deepest chasm showed perfect correspondence of stratification, conforming to the general dip, and nowhere displacement; and the bottom rock, so often dry and bare, was perhaps deeply eroded, but continuous from side to side, a portion of the yet undivided series lying below.

Newberry interpreted the valleys, cliffs, and plateaus of the region as evidence of a long period of erosion in which tremendous amounts of rock had been worn away, but he gave no explanation of *how* the Colorado River carved Grand Canyon.

Major John Wesley Powell won lasting fame as a result of his daring descent of the Colorado River by boat in 1869 and again in 1871. His were scientific explorations, and much worthwhile and illuminating information was gathered in spite of the hardships involved. Major Powell's narrative states:

All the mountain forms of this region are due to erosion; all the cañons, channels of living rivers and intermittent streams were carved by the running waters, and they represent an amount of corrasion difficult to comprehend. But the carving of the

A cut through eons of geologic time tells a story in the canyon walls, etched there by the classic forces of erosion—wind and water. Grand Canyon thunderstorms change the rock a particle at a time, carrying it away in rivulets of rain that form tributaries rushing to the river.

DAVID MUENCH

cañons and mountains is insignificant, when compared with the denudation of the whole area, as evidenced in the cliffs of erosion. Beds hundreds of feet in thickness and hundreds of thousands of square miles in extent, beds of granite and beds of schist, beds of marble and beds of sandstone, crumbling shales and adamantine lavas have slowly yielded to the silent and unseen powers of the air, and crumbled into dust and been washed away by the rains and carried into the sea by the rivers.

Clarence E. Dutton, a protégé of Major Powell, conducted geological studies of the Colorado Plateau region in the late 1800s and shared his mentor's belief that the Colorado River was older than the landforms or structures it crossed in descending to the sea. They thought that, prior to formation of the canyons, the river must have been well established in a route much like its present course, flowing across a vast, low-lying plain. They theorized that the river had many twists and bends in it, similar to those which other old rivers flowing through their broad valleys possessed.

Then uplift of the land occurred slowly, raising the entire southwestern part of the continent. The old river was rejuvenated and began to cut downward into the land. In the vicinity of today's Grand Canyon, a gentle doming or upwarp of the layers of the earth's crust took place as the Kaibab Plateau was elevated. The river, it was thought, was able to cut downward as fast as the land rose, thus entrenching itself even deeper. If the Kaibab Plateau had been elevated too rapidly it would have blocked the flow of the river and forced the Colorado to find another route.

Two cycles of erosion were contemplated in this theory—one in which the plateau surface was formed and a later one in which canyon-cutting in the plateau took place. For decades this theme and variations of it dominated explanations of how Grand Canyon—and other canyons of the Colorado and its tributaries—came to be.

SUGGESTED READING

HUGHES, J. DONALD. *In the House of Stone and Light, A Human History of the Grand Canyon*. Grand Canyon, Ariz.: Grand Canyon Natural History Ass'n., 1978.

IVES, JOSEPH C. *Report Upon The Colorado River of the West*. Washington, D.C.: Gov't. Printing Office, 1861.

POWELL, J. W. *Exploration of the Colorado River of the West and Its Tributaries*. Washington, D.C.: Government Printing Office, 1875.

STEGNER, WALLACE. *Beyond the Hundredth Meridian*. Boston: Houghton Mifflin Company, 1954.

THORNBURY, WILLIAM D. *Regional Geomorphology of the United States*. New York: John Wiley and Sons, Inc., 1965.

Even in this arid country, water collects—and heads toward the Colorado in many stunningly beautiful cuts, such as this one at Upper Deer Creek Falls, which one must hike to for the view. The water tumbles down to ultimately reach Lower Deer Creek Falls, a view that nearly every river runner stops to enjoy.

How was the Grand Canyon formed?

How and when the Colorado River became established in its present course remains a subject of continuing interest, study, and debate. What happened at Grand Canyon is related to many geologic events that occurred elsewhere on the Colorado Plateau and makes a story too complex for full treatment here. The geologic evidence available is subject to different interpretations; consequently, different theories have developed.

Some researchers thought the Colorado had developed its route to the sea while flowing across the softer rock formations that once covered the region and that it maintained this course as it cut deeper and encountered the more resistant structure of the Kaibab and other plateaus. Streams which have been lowered or let down in this manner across underlying ridges are said to be "superposed." Geologists later found conclusive evidence that the earth movements which created the Kaibab Plateau took place much earlier than formerly supposed; they actually began about sixty-five million years ago as part of a series of mountain-building events geologists call the *Laramide revolution.*

Waves and sun reveal another plane of the canyon's many-faceted personality.

There was no through-flowing Colorado River with an outlet to the Gulf of California at that time. Sediments deposited in freshwater lakes on the Colorado Plateau indicate the existence of a series of enclosed basins with interior drainage (no outlet for water). These were later drained by the Colorado River and its tributaries. Some scientists believe the Colorado might first have gained an outlet to the south and east, perhaps draining into the Gulf of Mexico, since high plateaus prevented it from flowing west. If so, the drainage was later terminated because of earth movements that caused uplift in the vicinity of today's Arizona-New Mexico boundary.

Recent studies of Colorado River delta deposits in the Imperial Valley of California support the idea that the river formerly emptied elsewhere. The delta deposits began to form about 5.5 million years ago and have been forming continuously since that time. Minerals and tiny fossils from the *Mancos shale,* a rock formation found mostly in northeastern Arizona and southwestern Colorado upstream from Grand Canyon, mark the sediments as coming from the Colorado Plateau east of the Kaibab Plateau.

The fortification basalt in the *Muddy Creek formation* downstream from Grand Canyon, through which the river cuts its valley, has been dated by radiometric methods as about ten million years in age. This formation is known to be older than the westward-flowing Colorado River. Thus the Colorado River has followed its present general course for not more than ten nor less than 5.5 million years, during which time the Grand Canyon must have been carved.

Stream-Piracy Theory

One group of geologists suggests that about thirty-five million years ago the Kaibab Plateau separated two river-drainage systems. One, the Hualapai drainage, ran southwestward to the Gulf of California from plateaus to the west of the Kaibab. The other was the ancestral Upper Colorado system, which drained southward into Arizona from Utah. This drainage may initially have had an outlet southeast to the Gulf of Mexico, later terminated by uplift of the land to the east, causing the formation of a large lake. Remnants of lake sediments deposited in this body of water have been named the *Bidahochi formation.*

The somber rock of steep canyon walls bears silent witness to an antiquity so profound that it cannot be grasped by human minds.

Boulders and debris that once were part of the canyon walls have been carried by the river and deposited at the mouths of its many side canyons. Here at Havasu Creek, boaters stop to prepare for a hike into the Havasupai Reservation to enjoy the spectacular falls and beautiful pools of Havasu Canyon.

ERNST HAAS

The western or Hualapai drainage gathered water over a wide area, and its headwaters gradually began to extend toward the east by headward erosion in the weak rocks which covered the plateau. It grew longer, slowly eating back into the western slope of the Kaibab upwarp until it finally crossed the southern margin of the plateau and captured the drainage of the Upper Colorado. Thus the Colorado River was born as a through-flowing stream from the Rocky Mountains to the Gulf of California.

Through stream piracy the alignment of the river was achieved, and it began to cut downward through thousands of feet of rock to create Grand Canyon. This event probably took place no earlier than ten million years ago, and the age of certain lava flows which cover river gravels west of Grand Canyon indicate the event was certainly at least 3.3 million years ago.

The foregoing explanation has been challenged on the basis that it violates a geological principle known as the "law of migrating divides,"

The Colorado and Little Colorado rivers join on the east side of the Kaibab Plateau. The manner in which Grand Canyon was carved through the southern end of the plateau remains a matter of conjecture and controversy among geologists.

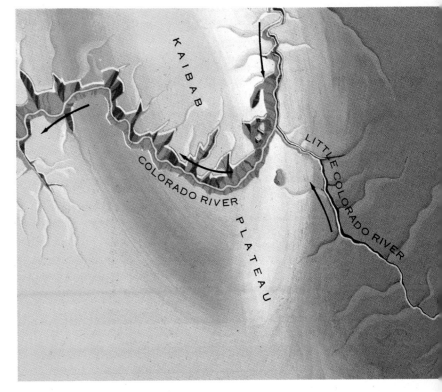

which holds that slopes which receive the most moisture and are steepest erode fastest. In this case it is assumed that the eastward-flowing streams eroded headward faster than westward-flowing drainages such as the Hualapai. Furthermore, analysis of the lake sediments which make up the Bidahochi formation indicates that the ancestral Colorado River came from a source predominantly northeastern rather than northwestern. Also, mid-Bidahochi sediments have been dated at 4.1 million years in age, a time when the Colorado River had already begun emptying into the Gulf of California.

Ancestral-Little-Colorado-River Theory

Some geologists believe that the ancestral river which began cutting Grand Canyon about twenty million years ago was either the San Juan or the Little Colorado. The Colorado itself is thought to have drained westward during this period from the Rocky Mountains into the Uinta Basin of Utah, where it was held captive in lakes. The Little Colorado was then a much larger stream because it drained a mountainous region in central Arizona. The establishment of this westward flow by superposition across the Kaibab Plateau would have required it to be, at the time, some 1,500 feet lower than some evidence indicates and to be subsequently uplifted that much or more. Evidence of this uplift is lacking.

The westward flow of the ancestral stream was later blocked by renewed uplift of the Kaibab Plateau. The waters were ponded to form a lake, and deposition of Bidahochi sediments took place. Later, only a few million years ago, the ancestral Colorado River joined the diminished Little Colorado and the San Juan to overflow through the partially excavated ancestral Grand Canyon.

This theory has been challenged on the grounds that it is more likely that the elevation of the Kaibab Plateau was 1,000 feet higher rather than 1,500 feet lower at the time the ancestral Grand Canyon is believed to have been cut. Basalt forming a cap on Red Butte near the South Rim of Grand Canyon has been dated by radiometric methods at

eight to ten million years, indicating that the softer rocks beneath the cap formed the general surface of the plateau at that time. Most of this material has since been eroded.

It seems certain that much research remains to be done before a theory can evolve upon which there will be general agreement. Such an explanation is bound to be extremely complicated, because so many new discoveries must be integrated with older information. The knowledge explosion makes us all too aware of how little we really know!

No matter how the Grand Canyon was formed, it is a fact, and it was produced by erosion. The river itself has carved a vertical distance of a mile into the earth's crust. Other forces of erosion have widened the canyon. They are not as dramatic as the mighty river, but their work is important nevertheless.

Expansion and contraction, caused by heat and cold, combine with wind and chemical action to weather the exposed rock surfaces and loosen bits of material which can then be moved. Rain falls from the sky and each droplet has the power to displace loose sand or soil. Floods course down side canyons, carrying debris toward the river. Snow falls on the South Rim in winter; it seldom accumulates to great depths, but during the heat of the day it melts and percolates into the surrounding rocks. Then at night, when temperatures drop, the water turns to ice, expanding and wedging rocks further apart.

Boulders and debris pour forth from side canyons
such as this one. The huge collection was brought
here and deposited by the flash floods that
occur erratically in the climate of the inner canyon.

Most of the streams which have carved side canyons are intermittent; others are spring-fed, carrying water all year. Many drainages have been formed along faults or fractures in the rock layers where the weakened rock has been worn away more easily. When floods roar down side canyons, they carry huge boulders as well as smaller debris to the Colorado River at the canyon bottom. The river, already laden with sand and silt, cannot remove this added material all at once. Roaring, leaping rapids are formed where the river channel is partially blocked.

Hard layers of rock in the canyon walls form cliffs; softer rocks form slopes. Cliffs retreat or are eroded by the falling of large blocks as softer rocks at the base are worn away, undermining the cliffs. Erosion takes place underground as well as on the earth's surface. Sinkholes in the limestone cover of the Kaibab Plateau and large caverns in the Redwall and Muav limestone layers of the canyon walls attest to the ever-present processes of solution and transportation of rock by water.

What is the future of Grand Canyon? It could become nearly a half mile deeper, since the river is still that high above sea level. If erosion continues unabated and new earth-building events do not occur, the canyon will certainly continue to grow wider. The cliffs will retreat and the rock layers forming canyon walls will erode bit by bit.

Ultimately, after many millions of years, the Grand Canyon may exist no more. A sluggish Colorado River may flow in wide loops and bends across a level plain, an erosion surface not unlike others that have left evidence of their passing in the walls of Grand Canyon.

SUGGESTED READING

BAARS, DONALD L. *Red Rock Country: The Geologic History of the Colorado Plateau.* New York: Doubleday & Co.; 1972.

HUNT, CHARLES B. "Grand Canyon and the Colorado River, Their Geologic History," *Geology of the Grand Canyon.* Flagstaff, Ariz.: Museum of Northern Arizona and Grand Canyon Natural History Ass'n. 2nd ed., 1976.

HUNT, CHARLES B. "Geologic History of the Colorado River." *The Colorado River Region and John Wesley Powell.* Wash., D.C.: U.S. Gov't. Printing Off., 1969.

McKEE, E. D.; WILSON, R. F.; BREED, W. J.; AND BREED, C. S. *Evolution of the Colorado River in Arizona.* Report of the Symposium on Cenozoic Geology of the Colorado Plateau in Arizona, August, 1964. Flagstaff, Arizona: Mus. of No. Ariz. Bull. No. 44, 1967.

MERRIAM, RICHARD, AND BANDY, ORVILLE L. "Source of Upper Cenozoic Sediments in Colorado Delta Region." *Journal of Sedimentary Petrology*, Vol. 35, No. 4, December, 1965.

Grand Canyon was cut through the southern slope of the Kaibab Plateau. The North Rim is hundreds of feet higher than the South Rim. Elevation of the plateau increases to 9,000 feet above sea level farther north. The North Rim climate is more severe than that of the South Rim, and snow builds to several feet deep in winter. When spring comes, the snow and ice melt rapidly and water flows southward off the plateau into the canyon, whereas drainage from the South Rim is to the south and actually away from the canyon in many places. The result is that Grand Canyon is being enlarged to the north much faster than to the south.

Sunrise bathes the canyon in a blood-red glow that intensifies
this well known profile at Yaki Point. The stark silhouette emphasizes
the awesomeness of the forces which carved the canyon out
of a plateau high above sea level.

Time and the Canyon Walls

Geologists have divided the history of the earth into four eras, each of which spans many millions of years. The first era is so much longer than the other three that it has been divided into two parts. We can then speak in terms of five "chapters" of geologic time. The evidence of the passage of these chapters is preserved extremely well in the Grand Canyon region; they can be "read"—in much the same manner as chapters in a book—if one understands the language. A few pages and many paragraphs are missing here and there, but the record in the rocks can nevertheless be tied together in a readable manner.

The first era, and the longest, represents the most ancient times and is called the Precambrian. It consists of Chapter I, the Early Precambrian, and Chapter II, the Late Precambrian. Chapter III is the Paleozoic era; Chapter IV, the Mesozoic era; and Chapter V, the Cenozoic era. Chapter V is still going on today, having lasted now for approximately sixty-five million years. An important thing to remember is that the Grand Canyon was carved in the Cenozoic era, probably in the last six million years, but the rocks which make up the canyon walls are a great deal older.

THE ROCKS AND EVENTS OF CHAPTER I

Rocks of Chapter I can easily be identified from the rim of Grand Canyon. They form the walls of the Inner Gorge, a canyon within the canyon. Its walls rise as much as 1,500 feet above river level. These rocks appear very dark and forbidding and give the impression of vertical layering. Seams of lighter-colored material appear here and there in the gorge.

The dark-colored Early Precambrian rocks were not always as we see them today. Some of them were originally laid down in horizontal layers, much like the upper layers of the canyon walls. Others were volcanic materials. The rock layers were many thousands of feet thick when something happened which permanently changed their nature:

The earth's crust was buckled and warped by

A seam of pink granite curves away from the river in a graceful arch that contrasts with the dark schist around it. Such seams are the result of intrusions into the older rock.

The Inner Gorge was carved in ancient schist and granite. On either side is a broad bench or platform, the Tonto Plateau. This aerial view from above the inner canyon looks eastward.

At the head of Hance Rapid, a basalt dike cuts through the Hakatai shale. A very thin intrusion underlies the more massive dike.

The geologic processes at work in the canyon have produced fascinating forms and colorations.

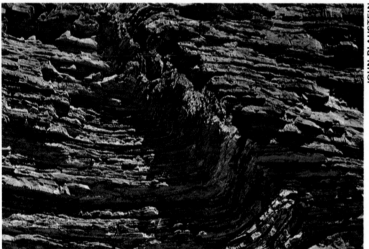

Tapeats sandstone was literally bent under the tremendous pressure of nature's forces at work.

tremendous internal forces, and a range of mountains was created where the horizontal rock layers had been. These mountains were probably as high as any in the world today, perhaps five or six miles high. This period of mountain building is called the *Arizonan* and *Mazatzal revolutions*.

Tremendous heat and pressure generated in the rocks as earth movements took place. The rocks recrystallized; they became changed or metamorphosed. Molten material from the interior of the earth penetrated into the base of the newly created mountain chain, forced its way into the rock, and then cooled and hardened.

The dark metamorphic rock which formed the mountains is called the *Vishnu group*, while the lighter-colored material (granite or pegmatite) is known as *Zoroaster gneiss*. These formations make up the walls of the Inner Gorge of the canyon today and probably extend thousands of feet below the present floor of Grand Canyon.

While the high mountains of Chapter I were being constructed, the most certain processes we know in nature were also at work. The mountains were assailed by the agents of erosion and were gradually, bit by bit, reduced to a plain. Only the roots of the mountain chain remained when the land slowly submerged beneath the advancing sea, marking the end of Chapter I in Grand Canyon's book of time.

How long ago did this take place?

Radiometric-age determinations on granite from the Inner Gorge indicate that mountain-building, with its accompanying metamorphism and intrusion, occurred about 1.7 billion years ago. The original Vishnu sediments are even older, so an estimate of two billion years in age seems reasonable. Chapter I came to an end more than 1.2 billion years ago.

Life may have existed during Chapter I, but no fossil traces have yet been found in these rocks.

Perhaps the heat and pressure which accompanied mountain-building erased all signs of life, for evidence of living things has been found in rocks of this age, and older, in other parts of the world.

Scientists have recovered traces of organisms, believed to be bacteria, and single-celled plants from the *Gunflint chert* of the Canadian shield; Their age is believed to be nearly two billion years.

Rocks, Fossils and Events of Chapter II

In the shallow water which covered eroded remnants of the Chapter I mountains, sediments began to accumulate. Inch upon inch, layer upon layer, the rocks of Chapter II were formed. Distant highlands were worn away and materials were transported to form the building stuff of rock layers at least two miles thick. The lowermost layer, deposited directly on the eroded surface of the schist, is called *Bass limestone*. Primitive plants played a part in building this formation. Many limestone reefs were formed through the agency of algae, and the peculiar, wavy-line structures in some parts of the rock represent the oldest known life recorded in Grand Canyon.

Geologists noticed a similarity between specimens from the Bass limestone of Grand Canyon and limestone being formed in modern times near Harpers Ferry, West Virginia. Bass limestone also preserves ripplemarks and mud cracks, which suggest that the deposit was formed under alternating shallow-water and mud-flat conditions.

New layers of sediment covered older ones. Immediately above the Bass limestone lies a brilliant vermilion rock, *Hakatai shale*, probably also formed under shallow-water conditions with occasional emergences. Ripplemarks, mudcracks,

These colorful, sloping rock layers, once horizontal, were tilted when the fault-block mountains of the Late Precambrian were formed. The horizontal layers of Paleozoic rock above them were deposited after the mountains had eroded. Hance Rapid lies far below the skyline perch of Solomon Temple.

A fault rises in a sweeping arc to separate the diabase sill and the Dox formation.

The river flows in wide loops and bends across an open canyon floor in the eastern end of Grand Canyon. These Late Precambrian rock layers were more than two miles thick at one time. Aerial view is to the northeast from above Hance Rapid.

TAD NICHOLS

and raindrop impressions attest to this origin. Next came deposits of quartz-sand grains tightly cemented to make a hard, resistant rock which stands as cliffs wherever it is exposed. The name *Shinumo quartzite* has been given this formation. It, too, contains ripplemarks and cross-bedded layers which suggest shallow-water deposition.

Still another layer, the *Dox formation,* was added, bearing evidence of a similar origin. During deposition of the Dox formation, molten material from a great depth was forced upward into the rock, where it either spread out between layers, penetrated cracks and cooled to form sills and dikes, or reached the surface as basalt flows. Still other rock layers accumulated, until the total thickness of Chapter II rocks was 12,000 feet or more. Evidence of simple plant life is found in these rocks, but animal fossils had not been satisfactorily demonstrated until the 1970s, when scientists reported the discovery of planktonic animal microfossils called "chitinozoans." Fossils of jellyfish, sea pens, and other primitive animals have been found in rocks of this age in Australia.

A tremendous span of time was required to build these rock formations, but dramatic events were still to unfold before Chapter II would come to an end. Forces and stresses within the earth re-

shaped the land, and another series of mountain ranges was formed. These ranges differed from the mountains of Chapter I. They were fault-block mountains. Zones of weakness or fractures in the earth's crust developed. Slippage or movement along these faults permitted some blocks to be elevated, their rock layers tilted at an angle, while other zones were lowered.

The basic character of the rock layers and their horizontal relationship to each other were preserved, however, since the great heat and pressure which altered or metamorphosed the rocks during Chapter I mountain-building were not present during formation of the Chapter II fault-block mountains. This period of mountain-building is called the *Grand Canyon revolution.*

Even as the mountains rose, erosion took its toll. The highlands were vigorously attacked, and as the rock wore away the landscape became more level. Finally, after millions of years, only a plain remained, with ridges and monadnocks of resistant rock rising here and there. In many places the entire 12,000-foot thickness of Chapter II rocks had been completely worn away, exposing the ancient schist of Chapter I. In a few places, tilted wedges of Late Precambrian formations remained. This situation prevailed at the end of the Pre-

cambrian era, approximately 600 million years ago. Chapters I and II in Grand Canyon's book of time were complete.

Today these Late Precambrian rocks are exposed along the South Kaibab and North Kaibab trails. The Bright Angel trail does not pass through these formations, but they can be seen nearby. Extensive outcrops of Chapter II formations are found in the remote Shinumo amphitheater to the west of Grand Canyon Village. These rocks also form the broad canyon floor in the eastern end of Grand Canyon. There, because of the relative weakness of the rocks, the river is twice as wide as

The "Bridge of Sighs," named by the late Emery Kolb on one of his early river trips, circa 1910, is the only natural bridge that can be seen in the canyon from the river.

The storms that hasten the erosional process drift into the canyon frequently. The magnitude of the canyon allows nature to create weather that is totally contained within the canyon walls. Violent storms may rage on one side while visitors bask in sunshine on the other.

These horizontal rock layers above the Inner Gorge were formed during the Paleozoic era (Chapter III). The contact between the bottom layer and the vertical schist of the Early Precambrian (Chapter I) is called the "great unconformity," since it demonstrates a gap in which nature first built mountains and then leveled them, erasing over a half-billion years of geologic history. Aerial view is toward Shoshone and Yaki points on the South Rim from above Vishnu Creek.

in the areas of resistant schist and granite of the Inner Gorge, and broad benches flank the stream.

CHAPTER III—THE PALEOZOIC ERA

The upper two-thirds of the canyon walls are composed of formations deposited during Chapter III. The Grand Canyon region was beneath the sea, covered by river flood plains, invaded by desert dunes, and affected by various other environments. During this time, erosion intervals produced several *unconformities,* or gaps in the record, which are now revealed in the canyon walls.

The first rock formation of Chapter III, *Tapeats sandstone,* was deposited along the margins of a sea which covered the eroded remnants of Chapter I

mountains. Here the rocks of Chapter III rest directly upon the rocks of Chapter I. The record of Chapter II, the Late Precambrian, is completely missing in many places in Grand Canyon.

The contact or plane between the Vishnu group and Tapeats sandstone is called the *great unconformity.* This represents a time interval here of over 500 million years! This was the length of time required to deposit the rock layers of Chapter II, elevate them as fault-block mountains, and then wear those mountains away. The great unconformity can be seen at a distance from many places on the canyon rims and can be inspected at close range below Indian Gardens on the Bright Angel trail.

The Tapeats sandstone is composed of strata ranging in character from coarse pebbles to fine sandstone; the formation averages about 200 feet thick in the central part of the Grand Canyon. Fossil shells, impressions of seaweed, and ripplemarks point to the nature of the sea margin in which it was deposited.

Above the Tapeats lies the *Bright Angel shale,* composed of greenish siltstone and shale which also was formed as a sea deposit and now averages about 400 feet in thickness. Fossils in this formation show that life was abundant in the sea. Typical forms are brachiopods (primitive shellfish), and peculiar crablike creatures (trilobites) which ruled the seas for hundreds of millions of years.

Bright Angel shale forms the Tonto Plateau, a broad bench or platform above the Inner Gorge of Grand Canyon. Under the surface, this formation constitutes an aquiclude, or barrier to the downward penetration of percolating groundwater. Very little surface water is found on the canyon rims. Rain or snow seeps into the porous rock and some water finally emerges as springs in the canyon walls above the Bright Angel shale from a sea-deposited limestone layer called the *Muav formation.* This rock layer averages 400 feet thick and constitutes a regional aquifer, or water-bearing for-

mation. It contains caverns created by percolating ground water, which dissolves the limestone and carries it away. Fossil trilobites and brachiopods are common in this gray- or buff-colored rock.

A period of emergence from the sea and erosion of the land surface followed deposition of the Muav formation, leaving an unconformity. Channels or hollows formed on the erosion surface were later filled with a lavender-colored sea deposit called *Temple Butte limestone.* The fossils of animals with backbones are found in this formation. Bony

The Bright Angel shale is from a time when the sea covered Grand Canyon. This fossilized trilobite offers mute but indisputable evidence of that period in the canyon's history.

These diagrams illustrate the most important geological events which have taken place in the Grand Canyon region. A story of two billion years of earth's history has been reconstructed from evidence preserved in the rocks. Roman numerals indicate the chapters in which the events occurred, beginning with the oldest rocks and ending with the carving of the canyon.

CHAPTER I ROCKS

1. (I) Sediments and volcanic lavas accumulated in horizontal layers totaling thousands of feet in thickness.

2. (I) Rock layers were folded and meta- morphosed as a mountain range formed. Molten material invaded from below.

6. (II) The mountains were eroded to a plain. Only wedge-shaped remnants forming ridges were left.

CHAPTER III ROCKS

7. (III) Layers of sediment 4,000 feet thick were deposited. Subsequent erosion intervals left gaps in the record.

Viewed from Havasu Point on the West Rim, the limestone cliffs of the Redwall formation stand as monumental buttresses against time and weather. The red color actually comes from the iron oxide of the Supai formation, which washes over it from above.

TAD NICHOLS

3. (I) High mountains were eroded to a plain near sea level. Only the roots of mountains remained.

4. (II) The plain submerged, layers of sediment 12,000 feet thick were deposited, and molten material was injected.

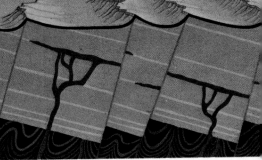

5. (II) Horizontal rock layers were broken and tilted as fault-block mountains were formed.

8. (IV) Sediments 4,000 to 8,000 feet thick accumulated, covering the Chapter III rock.

9. (V) Erosion removed all but a thin covering of Chapter IV rock, and the Colorado River established westward drainage.

10. (V) The downcutting river exposed ancient rocks. Remnants of Chapter IV rock remained. Volcanism occurred in the last million years.

plates or scales of an armored fish were preserved along with corals and brachiopods. A pocket of Temple Butte limestone occurs along the South Kaibab trail.

After an erosion interval, the next formation was deposited: the *Redwall limestone.* Abundant fossils of sea creatures such as corals, brachiopods, and crinoids (sea lilies) attest to its marine origin. The Redwall forms an impressive cliff averaging 550 feet high. Many caverns occur in this formation. The characteristic red color of the cliff is deceptive; the natural color of the limestone is gray. The surface of the cliff is stained by red iron oxide washed down from the *Supai formation* above. In the places where the overlying formation has been eroded away and no longer supplies the red "paint," Redwall limestone weathers to a gray color.

Another erosion interval followed deposition of the Redwall (thus creating another gap in the record). Then the land subsided and deposition of the Supai formation took place. The limey lower part of this formation was probably formed in a shallow retreating sea, whereas the sandy upper parts were deposited by rivers. Land plants grew near the water.

Four-footed animals, probably amphibians which lived both in and out of the water, left tracks along the muddy banks of streams. The tracks were covered with sand that was eventually cemented by water-borne minerals and hardened to rock. Erosion later exposed the footprints to view. No bones have been found, but one can surmise a

great deal about these creatures from studying only their tracks.

These tracks are close together, indicating short legs, and are deeply pressed into the rock (which once was mud), evidence that these creatures were heavy bodied. Between the right and left tracks of one variety are traces of drag marks, indicating that these creatures probably had tails. Scientists theorize that these animals looked somewhat like modern-day alligators or crocodiles.

The Supai formation appears as a stepped slope in the canyon walls just above the Redwall cliff. It averages nearly 1,000 feet thick and is a red color because of the iron oxides it contains. Erosion altered the surface of the Supai formation before the next rock layer was deposited and thus created still another unconformity. Then Hermit shale was deposited by freshwater streams as mud and clay. Iron compounds account for the deep-red color which it shares with the underlying Supai formation.

Mud cracks and ripplemarks indicate shallow-water deposition. Fossils in this rock include delicate impressions of ferns, cone-bearing plants, and insect wings. The footprints of small salamander-like animals are also preserved. The formation averages 300 feet thick in eastern Grand Canyon, and the fossils it contains give evidence of a semi-arid climate at the time of its origin.

Coconino sandstone overlies the Hermit shale. Windblown sand gathered into shifting desert dunes, which covered thousands of square miles. Crossbedded layers of sand resulting from the

Overleaf: Sunset on Grand Canyon; photo by Ray Atkeson

shifting winds can readily be observed along all canyon trails. The formation is 300 feet thick in parts of eastern Grand Canyon and less than 100 feet in the Toroweap Valley of western Grand Canyon. Coconino sandstone forms an imposing white- or buff-colored cliff about 600 feet below the rims of the canyon. Fossil footprints of primitive reptiles are preserved in the sand, and in a few places the trails of insects, scorpions, and worms are found.

A warm, shallow sea encroached upon the desert dunes, eroding away their tops and flattening the surface. The *Toroweap formation*, consisting of red and yellow sandstones at top and bottom with a gray limestone between, was deposited in this sea. The formation is more than 250 feet thick and contains fossils of brachiopods and mollusks, which indicate abundant marine life, left

by the Toroweap Sea as it retreated and then disappeared.

At still another time, marine waters inundated the Grand Canyon region and the Kaibab Sea advanced across the area. The uppermost 300 feet of rock in the canyon wall consists of a massive, creamy-white limestone rock called the *Kaibab formation*. It contains many fossils of sea organisms, mostly brachiopods but including corals, sea-lilies or crinoids, sponges, and shark teeth. Today's rim-rock, Kaibab limestone, was the last formation deposited in this region during the Paleozoic era, Chapter III.

About 230 million years ago Chapter III came to an end. At that time the newly deposited Kaibab formation was at sea level or below; but now, in some places, it is as much as 9,000 feet above sea level!

ED COOPER

From the North Rim, the Coconino sandstone of the Paleozoic era rises in sheer cliffs to an imposing height of 300 feet capped by the dark Toroweap formation. The wide variety of marine-life fossils found in these rocks were left behind as the ancient Toroweap Sea receded millions of years ago. The San Francisco peaks near Flagstaff appear on the distant horizon.

CHAPTER IV—THE MESOZOIC ERA

We have said that rocks representing nearly two billion years and five chapters of earth history are present in the Grand Canyon region. Yet upon reaching the canyon rimrock of Chapter III we have more or less run out of rock! Rocks of Chapter IV, the Mesozoic era, once covered this region completely, in layers totaling perhaps 4,000 to 8,000 feet in thickness. These rocks have since been eroded away, but we know that they were here because remnants were left behind.

Such a remnant is Cedar Mountain, near Desert View and the eastern boundary of the park. It is composed of the red sandstones and shales of the *Moenkopi formation*. The mountain is capped by a resistant gravel-layer called the *Shinarump conglomerate*.

These rocks, and some others which formerly covered them, were not marine in origin. Some consist of river-borne mud and gravel, others of windblown sand. Another remnant of Mesozoic era rock forms Red Butte about fifteen miles south of Grand Canyon Village. There, a cap of Chapter V lava rock protected the softer material beneath from rapid erosion.

The Painted Desert to the east of Grand Canyon was formed in Chapter IV rock, and so were the Echo and Vermilion cliffs to the northeast. Zion Canyon and the cliffs of southern Utah to the north were also carved in rock of this age. Is it, then, so hard to believe that these formations were once continuous and covered the Grand Canyon area?

The Mesozoic era is known as the "Age of Reptiles." This was the time when dinosaurs roamed the land. Tracks made by these creatures

THE GRAND CANYON

Length:	280 miles (450 kilometers), measured along the Colorado River.
Width:	4 to 18 miles (6.5 to 29 kilometers), with an average width of 9 miles (14.5 kilometers).
Depth:	Average, vertical, 1 mile (1.6 kilometers or 1,609 meters). From North Rim: 5,700 feet (1,750 meters). From South Rim: 4,500 feet (1,380 meters).
Elevations:	Difference between North Rim and South Rim developed areas, 1,200 feet (366 meters). North Rim about 8,200 feet (2,500 meters). South Rim about 7,000 feet (2,135 meters). Tonto Plateau about 4,000 feet (1,220 meters). Canyon Floor at Kaibab Suspension Bridge 2,500 feet (760 meters).

THE COLORADO RIVER

Length:	About 1,450 miles (2,333 kilometers). In Grand Canyon National Park, 280 miles (450 kilometers). 1,360 miles in U.S. and 90 miles in Mexico. 19 major canyons in the river's course.
Watershed:	River and its tributaries drain land area of over 240,000 square miles.
Width:	Average is about 300 feet (90 meters).
Descent:	From 10,000 feet (3,050 meters) to sea level. The river drops 2,220 feet (670 meters) in elevation in Grand Canyon National Park.
Rapids:	There are about 365 rapids along the river's length, with 70 major ones in Grand Canyon.

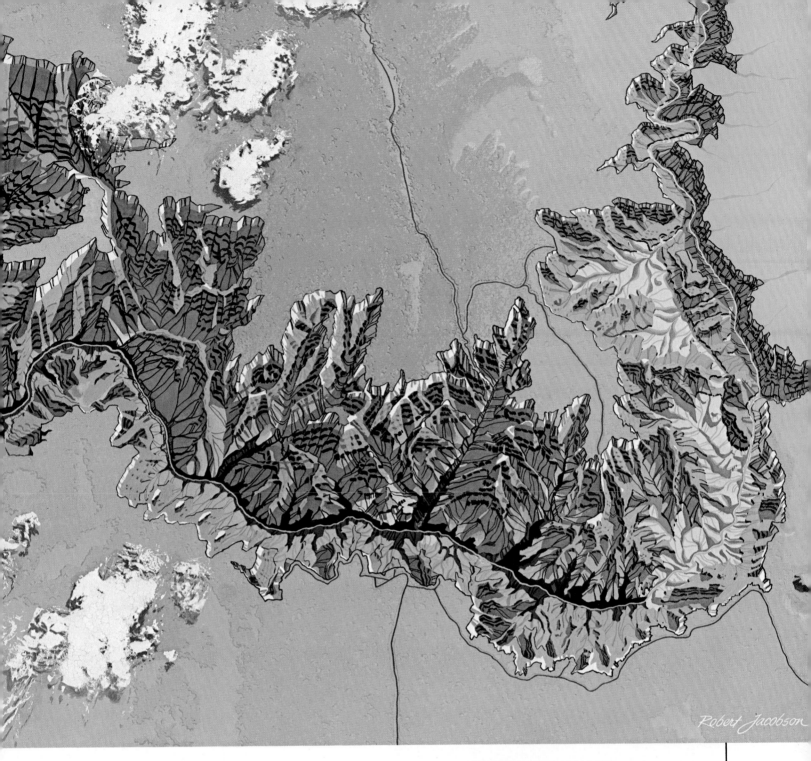

GRAND CANYON NATIONAL PARK

Originally established February 26, 1919.

Enlargement and present boundaries established by Act of Congress signed by President Gerald R. Ford January 3, 1975.

Administered by the National Park Service, United States Department of the Interior.

North Rim is open mid-May to mid-October.

South Rim is open all year.

Park includes 1,904 square miles or 1,218,375 acres.

The park is part of the Colorado Plateau physiographic province which covers about 130,000 square miles in parts of Utah, Colorado, New Mexico, and Arizona.

Studies of geologic processes, rocks, and fossils at this location have yielded much information about earth history.

INTERPRETING THE MAP

Chapter I Rocks (Lower Precambrian or Archean). Layers once horizontal are now vertical and changed by heat and pressure. Composed of dark schist and pink granite. Two billion years old.

Chapter II Rocks (Upper Precambrian or Algonkian). Layers once horizontal are now tilted at an angle. Composed of limestone, sandstone, and shale.

Chapter III Rocks (Paleozoic era). Layers are horizontal and form majority of canyon walls. Sedimentary in origin.

Chapter IV Rocks (Mesozoic era). Only small remnants are left at Grand Canyon, but these rocks once covered the entire region in a mile-thick layer.

Chapter V Rocks (Cenozoic era). Lavas are from volcanic activity about a million years ago.

Vulcan's Throne on the canyon rim is a recent cinder cone; the flows of lava in the canyon wall are even younger than the cone itself. Sometime within the last ten to twenty thousand years, these flows poured down from Mount Trumbull, higher up on the plateau.

are found today in the rocks near Tuba City on the Navajo Indian Reservation. Chapter IV ended about sixty-five million years ago.

CHAPTER V—THE CENOZOIC ERA

During all of Chapter V, the Cenozoic era, the Grand Canyon region has been above sea level. Some freshwater-lake deposits are preserved in surrounding areas but none are found in Grand Canyon National Park. In southern Utah the *Claron* (formerly Wasatch) *formation* was deposited, later to be sculpted into the colorful and fantastic forms visitors see in Bryce Canyon National Park.

The *Bidahochi formation* was deposited east of Grand Canyon when the waters of ancestral Colorado Plateau streams were temporarily ponded. To the west of Grand Canyon other lake deposits of

As the lava flows cooled, they formed huge, elongated, crystalline blocks. Eons of time have eroded the protective surfaces away to expose their massive shapes. An occasional cactus finds a receptive niche in which to live.

"Angel's Window" on the North Rim provides a lofty perch from which to view the canyon. Cedar Mountain, the solitary remnant of Mesozoic-era rock which formerly covered this region, is silhouetted against the skyline. The river below cuts its way through rock laid down billions of years ago in the Precambrian era.

DAVID MUENCH

limited extent also were accumulated during Chapter V. But the dominant process of Chapter V at Grand Canyon is the widespread erosion that has taken place. Thousands of feet of Mesozoic-era-rock formations have been stripped away, and in the last few million years the canyons have been cut and the earth sculpted as we see it today.

One last violent series of episodes did take place in Cenozoic time, however. Starting slightly more than one million years ago, after Grand Canyon was carved to within fifty feet or so of its present depth, molten rock from deep in the earth spewed forth. Volcanoes were born; lava poured down canyon walls and dammed the river in several places to create lakes. Heights of the lava dams varied from about 100 to 2,300 feet above the present river level. Water impounded behind the highest dams backed up through both Grand and Marble canyons.

Several periods of volcanic activity in this region are indicated by lava flows of different ages. South of Grand Canyon, volcanism built the San Francisco Peaks and hundreds of smaller cones near Flagstaff, Arizona. The San Francisco volcanic field covers about 3,000 square miles. Indians were living nearby at the time of the most recent eruptions; cinders and ashes from Sunset Crater covered their homes. The time of this event, determined by tree-ring dating of timbers used in construction, was about A.D. 1064.

Chapter V is known as the "Age of Mammals." Although evidence is scant, we do know that camels, horses, sloths, and mammoths once inhabited this region and later became extinct. Today many kinds of animals are found in and around Grand Canyon, but man—the highest form of life—was among the most recent arrivals. He dominates the planet Earth and turns resources to his benefit with an ever-expanding technology.

But, lest we think that nature no longer has a place in the scheme of things, let us view man's time on the earth against the backdrop of the two billion years of earth's history recorded in Grand Canyon's rocks. To make this comparison more understandable, imagine a compression of the entire two billion years into one twenty-four-hour day starting at midnight. Man is not here for breakfast the next morning and the rocks of Chapter I are still being formed. By lunchtime Chapter II begins and those primitive water plants called algae appear, but not man. At dinner time Chapter III is underway and the seas teem with marine organisms, but no land plants or animals exist. As the evening hours pass, generations of amphibians,

K. C. DEN DOOVEN

Although we sometimes think of geology as having happened millions of years ago, it is actually a fascinating process that is continuously going on beneath and around us. To illustrate: The horizontal bands on the sandbar were made in June of 1965 when the Bureau of Reclamation released an extremely large flow of water at Glen Canyon Dam. Two weeks later this photograph was taken. The rocks, which clearly straddle these bands, fell from the canyon walls sometime within the intervening two weeks. The shape of Grand Canyon is constantly changing!

In the lower canyon, visitors can see an interesting phenomenon. The small pebbles atop these whimsical little cones have actually saved the soft earth beneath them from the fate of the surrounding soil, which was washed away by rainwater.

GARY LADD

reptiles, pines, and ferns live and die; finally the dinosaurs become extinct as birds and mammals appear.

The carving of Grand Canyon begins about two and a half to four minutes before midnight. But ancient man does not enter the picture until about one million years ago (on the African continent), or forty-three seconds before midnight in the very last minute of our twenty-four-hour day! And, if one wishes to avoid controversy over exactly when and where man first appeared and his subsequent migrations, we might consider only his recorded history, which spans the last 5,000 years. This interval makes up the last one-fifth of a second in an eventful twenty-four hours. Man really hasn't been around very long at all!

SUGGESTED READING

BLOESER, B.; SCHOPF, J. W.; HORODYSKI, R. J.; AND BREED, W. J. "Chitinozoans from the Late Precambrian Chuar Group of the Grand Canyon, Arizona." *Science*, Vol. 195, No. 4279, February 18, 1977.

BREED, WILLIAM J. *Northern Arizona During the Age of Dinosaurs*. Flagstaff, Ariz.: Mus. of No. Ariz., 1968.

McKEE, EDWIN D. *Ancient Landscapes of the Grand Canyon Region*. Flagstaff, Arizona: Northland Press, 1959.

HAMBLIN, W. K., AND BEST, M. G. "The Western Grand Canyon District." *Guidebook to the Geology of Utah*, No. 23. Salt Lake City: Utah Geological Society, 1970.

Autumn adds her brilliant splashes of color to the gray sculptured forms gracing the walls of the North Rim's Point Sublime.

DARWIN VAN CAMPEN

41

Fossils

Fossils are ancient plant and animal remains or impressions preserved by any natural means. Even the hardened footprint or trail of an organism is a fossil. Some fossils are extremely small and can be studied only with the aid of the microscope, but others are very large indeed. A good example of the latter would be a dinosaur skeleton. Living things which have hard parts—bones, scales, or wood—leave better fossil records than those which are soft.

One of the conditions necessary for fossilization is the rapid natural burial of the evidence to protect it from weathering or decay. In some environments, parts of actual remains may be preserved for long periods of time. After an organism is covered, the process of petrifaction can begin. Ground water carries mineral material in solution, which fills in pores or spaces and gradually converts the specimen to stone. Water may also dissolve the original substance and replace it with a different kind of mineral; most fossils weigh considerably more than the original organism.

Imprints of leaves or animal tracks were preserved when the softer material into which they were pressed hardened, due to cementing by water-borne minerals and pressure from the overlying rock. Pressure and movement in the earth's crust frequently distort or break fossils, making them more difficult to interpret.

A fossil record of life through the ages has been preserved in Grand Canyon's walls. Marine and freshwater sediments provided excellent environments for preserving evidences of life. The rocks at the canyon bottom are about two billion years old and have yielded no evidence of ancient life. The younger rock layers above them preserve traces of primitive plants. Still higher up the canyon walls, the rock layers are progressively younger, and the fossils they contain show the development of life from simple to complex forms.

The north wall of Grand Canyon, as viewed from Yavapai Point, is a remarkable illustration of the record which the rocks have written upon the face of the earth.

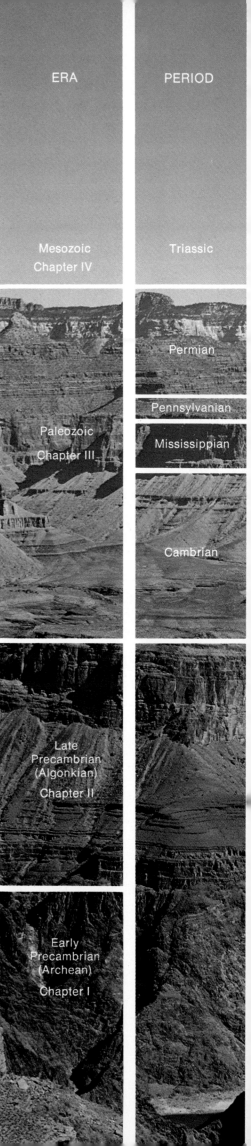

ERA

PERIOD

Mesozoic
Chapter IV

Triassic

Permian

Pennsylvanian

Paleozoic
Chapter III

Mississippian

Cambrian

Late
Precambrian
(Algonkian)

Chapter II

Early
Precambrian
(Archean)

Chapter I

FORMATION

KAIBAB
TOROWEAP
COCONINO
HERMIT

SUPAI

REDWALL

MUAV

BRIGHT ANGEL

TAPEATS

SHINUMO

HAKATAI

BASS

VISHNU

Reptile tracks in
Coconino sandstone

Productid brachiopod
from Kaibab limestone

Seedfern leaf and insect wing from Hermit shale

Bellerophontid snail
from Redwall limestone

Arthrodiran fish plate
from Temple Butte limestone

Amphibian or reptile tracks
in Supai formation

Trilobite from
Bright Angel shale

Algal reef
from Bass limestone

Modern algal reef from
Harpers Ferry, West Virginia

43

Canyon moods vary with the time of day, season of year, and weather conditions. The canyon is at its best before midmorning, at eventide, or after a storm. During the middle of the day, lighting is rather flat, broken only by cloud shadows. In the evening, darkness slowly climbs the sheer walls, cloaking the canyon with a mantle of mystery and quiet. The interplay of light and shadow accentuates a multitude of fine details in form and sculpture.

The Canyon Today

All the elements of the Grand Canyon scene, except the magnificent earth sculpture of ancient rocks, are very recent indeed. Plants and animals give the landscape life and show the great diversity that is present in nature.

And what a variety of life there is! A thousand species of plants are found in the park. Large animals—such as Rocky Mountain mule deer, desert bighorn sheep, mountain lion, bobcat, and coyote —are found in the canyon or on the rims. These and smaller squirrels, mice, bats, and other forms make a total of seventy-five kinds of mammals inhabiting Grand Canyon. The flashing wings and pleasant sounds of about 230 kinds of birds add interest to the canyon scene. Variety also extends to the amphibians and reptiles; forty-three species are present here. Some sixteen species of fish have been identified from the Colorado River and its tributaries in the park.

Changes in elevation from plateau heights to canyon floor influence temperature and rainfall, and slopes vary in exposure to sunlight. Different climates or environments are thus created, which in turn favor varied plant and animal associations.

PHOTOS BY DAVID MUENCH

Winter is perhaps the most beautiful season in the canyon. The snow's whiteness highlights the rich colors, and fog descends into the canyon to fill it with an ethereal mist, creating effects that exhilarate and inspire the fortunate spectator.

46

A cautious fox peeks from a rocky crevice.

JOHN RUNNING

JOHN RUNNING

Wild burros amble along the edge of the river.

Egrets enjoy the solitude of the inner canyon.

JOHN BLAUSTEIN

In the Grand Canyon region a 1,000-foot increase in elevation is roughly equivalent in its effect on climate to a move northward of 300 miles with no increase in altitude.

The higher portions of the Kaibab Plateau north of the canyon have an average annual precipitation of twenty-six inches and support forests of spruce, fir, and quaking aspen. Porcupines and spruce squirrels are common here and at slightly lower elevations where a transition forest of ponderosa pine is found.

Notable residents of the ponderosa pines are the tassel-eared squirels, which depend largely upon the twigs and cones of these trees for their food. The tassel-eared squirrel of the North Rim has an all-dark body and an all-white tail. This rare creature is known as the "Kaibab squirrel" and is found only in the ponderosa-pine forests of the Kaibab Plateau. The squirrel from the opposite side of the canyon is much like the Kaibab squirrel

and yet is quite different. The South Rim's Abert squirrel lives in the pine forests of the southern Rocky Mountain region and northern Mexico. It is a gray squirrel with white underparts and a long tail which is white underneath and gray above.

The lower plateau and rim areas have an average rainfall of about sixteen inches yearly. They are covered with a pygmy forest of pinyon pine and Utah juniper. Changes in climate are subtle but sure. Descending to the floor of the canyon, one finds a desert region with less than ten inches of rainfall each year. Vegetation is sparse, but cactus, agave, and blackbrush dot the landscape; willows and cottonwoods grow along stream courses. The spotted skunk, Grand Canyon rattlesnake, and chuckwalla lizard also inhabit the region.

Non-native, wild burros are common in central and western Grand Canyon; they range from the rim to the river. Although these creatures are very appealing, it should be remembered that the

The canyon may seem to be a harsh environment in which to live, but many animals and birds find it a desirable home where they can find adequate food. The wild burros are the only non-native species here, introduced in earlier years as pack animals for the mines.

A hummingbird taps the nectar of a thistle bloom.

Bighorn sheep range from river to rim.

The Grand Canyon rattlesnake is a subspecies of western rattlesnake.

An alert collared lizard watches from the canyon floor.

Bathers frolic in the beautiful blue-green travertine pools below Havasu Falls within the Havasupai Indian Reservation. Mooney Falls (right) is another of the three major falls in Havasu Canyon. Access to these falls is generally gained from the river, although those who wish to better observe the ways of the Havasupai may get there by muleback, hike into the reservation, or arrive by helicopter.

preservation of natural conditions among native species of plants and animals may necessitate the removal of the burro from this environment.

The Grand Canyon region encompasses climates ranging from hot desert to arctic cold, if the San Francisco Mountains, with their maximum elevation of 12,670 feet, are included. The vertical change in elevation from canyon floor to mountain peak exceeds 10,000 feet within a horizontal distance of fifty miles!

NATIVE AMERICANS

Canyon country is Indian country! The cultures of prehistoric and modern Indians are imprinted on this sculptured land. Hundreds of prehistoric Indian sites are found on the rims and in the canyon. Tusayan Ruin near Desert View formerly housed twenty-five or thirty people and was built about A.D. 1185.

Today's Indians occupy much land around Grand Canyon. The Navajo live on a sixteen-million-acre reservation which adjoins the eastern boundary of the park. The Navajo, still partly nomadic, are herdsmen who live in small groups and graze livestock over the far reaches of their reservation. Navajo ancestors migrated south from Canada. In the center of the Navajo nation lies the 631-thousand-acre Hopi Indian Reservation. The Hopi people are farmers whose ancestors occupied the northern southwest for many centuries. They live together in villages. The Hopi pueblo of Oraibi is about 800 years old, the oldest continuously occupied settlement on the continent.

About 300 Havasupai Indians live in a spectacular side canyon thirty-five miles west of Grand Canyon Village. Their steep-walled canyon home is accessible only by trail. Fertile fields are watered from spring-fed Havasu Creek. The name *Havasupai* means "people of the blue-green water" and relates to the color of the stream. The waterfalls and delicate, terraced pools along the creek add to the beauty of their canyon home.

The flowers within Grand Canyon
are exquisitely beautiful, although
the lack of a continuing supply
of moisture limits their numbers.
Cacti, in its wide variety of forms,
are ideally suited to the landscape
and arid climate of the canyon.

BILL BELKNAP

BILL BELKNAP

Cacti blooms— *—delicate beauty among practical spines*

JOHN BLAUSTEIN

Datura, fragile counterpoint to massive rock

PATRICIA CAULFIELD

K. C. DEN DOOVEN

Yucca along the river bank

Ocotillo, also called "candlewood"

Agave (century plant) in full bloom

EARLY SETTLERS

Explorers made the great canyon known, and soon prospectors began to search for precious metals in the ancient rocks exposed by erosion. But treasure of the kind they sought eluded them.

The first mining and tourist developments at Grand Canyon were made near Grandview Point, when John Hance arrived about 1883. He scratched a crude trail to his asbestos claims at the canyon bottom, built a cabin on the rim, and by 1886 was advertising in the Flagstaff newspaper a guide service for visitors. His were the first tourist facilities. A short time later William Wallace Bass began a similar type of operation at Havasupai Point, about thirty miles west of Grandview.

W. H. Ashurst, Pete Berry, Ralph and Niles Cameron, and others located copper claims on Horseshoe Mesa in 1890 and 1891. They built the Grandview trail and hauled out the ore with pack animals. Members of this same group of pioneers also improved an old Indian path eleven miles to the west which led to Indian Gardens and named it "Bright Angel Trail."

A hotel was built at Grandview Point in 1892 and stagecoaches started scheduled passenger service from Flagstaff the same year. (The fare was $20.) The Santa Fe Railroad reached the South Rim in 1901, and as new facilities were developed at the railhead, Grandview's popularity waned. Grand Canyon Village became the center of activities.

Opportunities were available then, as now, for visitors to satisfy their desire to see the canyon's moods and features from rim drives and along inner-canyon trails. Canyon hiking or mule travel has provided many memorable experiences for adventurous visitors.

In recent years flights over the canyon and boat trips down the Colorado River have become readily available. The traverse of Grand Canyon by boat is a superb adventure requiring about ten days' time and a love of the great outdoors. The unknowns, fears, and dangers that Major Powell and other river-running pioneers faced have been greatly reduced by competent expedition leaders and improved equipment, but the thrills and scenery remain.

Central Section, Grand Canyon National Park

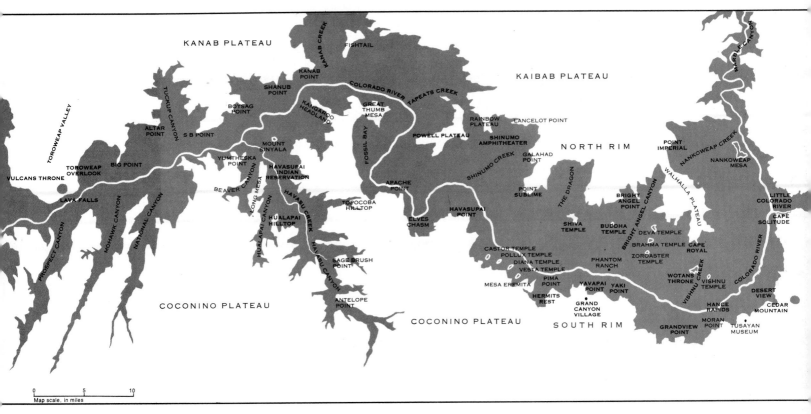

Establishing a Park

Pioneers gained a foothold at the canyon and worked to develop its mineral, forest, and recreation potential, but the movement to preserve the canyon, for the benefit of all the American people, started elsewhere.

In 1882, 1883, and 1886, Senator Benjamin Harrison of Indiana introduced bills to make Grand Canyon a national park. All failed—because of opposition by those who feared their economic interests would be damaged. But Harrison persisted, and in 1893, as President of the United States, he established by proclamation the Grand Canyon Forest Reserve. The area remained open for mining, lumbering, and hunting.

President Theodore Roosevelt visited Grand Canyon in 1903. Inspired by his experience, he established the Grand Canyon Game Reserve for the protection of wild animals as well as the land (in 1906) and the Grand Canyon National Monument (in 1908).

The Congressional act which established Grand Canyon National Park was signed by President Woodrow Wilson on February 26, 1919. A new Grand Canyon National Monument adjoining the park on the west was established by President Herbert Hoover on December 22, 1932. President Lyndon B. Johnson established the fifty-mile-long Marble Canyon National Monument by proclamation on January 20, 1969.

Legislation enlarging Grand Canyon National Park was signed by President Gerald R. Ford on January 3, 1975. The bill combined the existing Marble Canyon and Grand Canyon national monuments with the park and added portions of Glen Canyon and Lake Mead national recreation areas and other public lands. Some 83,809 acres of former park land were deleted to enlarge the Havasupai Indian Reservation. The resulting park consists of 1,218,375 acres of scenic beauty.

Far-sighted men have played important roles in making Grand Canyon available to all people as part of our national heritage. As Theodore Roosevelt said, on his first trip to Grand Canyon: *"Do nothing to mar its grandeur . . . keep it for your children, your children's children, and all who come after you, as the one great sight which every American should see."*

Matkatamiba Canyon in the lower end of Grand Canyon

Below the South Rim overlooks, out of sight except for an occasional glimpse, the Colorado enters its Upper Granite Gorge, where stark, black walls meet rushing water for forty miles.

The river lies in sandstones and limestones along much of its way, rocks which are more easily cut away and thus impede the river less. Although the river still runs with urgency in such places, it is not as turbulent as in other areas.

The River Below

Not content with what it has already achieved, the great Colorado River still exerts its erosive powers on the canyon floor. Chemical weathering is the dominant force at work. The torrent moves in swirls and eddies, keeping its load of sand and silt suspended. It also carries dissolved compounds and some larger particles which may drop to the channel bed to be moved downstream by rolling or bouncing. Tributary drainages bring boulders and sediments into the relentless fow. In the places where these materials cannot be used as fast as they are brought to the river, the water tumbles over and around them, forming rapids that offer challenges to adventurous individuals.

Through the spring and summer months, thousands of people join the boating expeditions through Grand Canyon offered by experienced river guides. The depths of the inner gorge give these adventurers a perspective of Grand Canyon which is not attainable in any other way. And it provides them with a new awareness of the power of the river.

The vertical columns of cascading water contrast dramatically to the layers upon layers of horizontal rock and their sparse vegetation. Wherever the water flows, trees and other plant life grow in abundance. Some of these waterfalls spill directly into pools near the river's edge; others lie hidden in side canyons which can only be reached after a hard climb on foot.

Thunder River Falls

Today, increasing use of the river is creating serious problems. In some places the impact of human use is greater than the fragile resources there can sustain without impairment. To illustrate the magnitude of the problem: In the eighty-two years from 1867 through 1948, only ninety-six people traveled through Grand Canyon on the Colorado River. In the next thirteen years, 1949 through 1961, a total of 1,039 people made the trip. Only five years later, in 1966, 1,067 passengers "ran the river" in a single year. The tide has continued to mount; by the mid-1970s, about 15,000 people were accommodated annually. We are often reluctant to acknowledge that there are limits to healthy growth, but here is a situation that demands our attention.

Prior to the closure of Glen Canyon Dam in 1963, the untamed Colorado River was given to periodic, raging floods which flushed sandy beaches and gravel bars clear of debris and hampered the growth of permanent vegetation along the river banks. Camping places were many, and driftwood was plentiful. The controlled flow of the river today has resulted in pronounced changes. Sand beaches tend to be washed away, and river banks are covered with vegetation. Some rapids are growing larger because the flooding of tributary streams carries more debris to the river than it can remove. The number of stopping places for visitors is limited. Camping, picnicking, trampling, littering, and other activities cause degradation of the environment.

It is a curious contradiction that the appreciation of the joys of river-running by greater numbers of visitors threatens to impair the quality of the resources they use and the experience they seek at Grand Canyon.

SUGGESTED READING

BELKNAP, BUZZ. *Grand Canyon River Guide*. Boulder City, Nevada: Westwater Books, 1969.

Upper Deer Creek

GARY LADD

The People's Heritage

There is still much that man can learn from nature if the great outdoor laboratories can be preserved unimpaired. And there is much that man can learn about himself. We are told that human judgment is based upon comparisons. Therefore, judgment can be no better than the experience upon which it rests. If men are deprived of the opportunity to witness natural beauty, observe native plants and animals, study undisrupted geologic features and processes, breathe clear air, or drink unpolluted water, then how valid will their judgments of such things be?

Americans of today must provide the coming generations with opportunities to experience nature. We are obligated to preserve natural wonders such as Grand Canyon for the people of the entire world. This wonderful heritage of ours involves great responsibilities towards people of the future as well as great opportunities for us today.

You have seen Grand Canyon with your mind as well as with your eyes, but this is an opportunity to use your other senses as well.

Go out along the canyon rim alone to watch dark shadows climb the colored walls as the sun drops to the horizon. Think about the eons of time represented by rock formations exposed to your view and the fossil record of life through the ages they contain. Feel the bite of the wind on your cheeks and listen for the sound of distant rapids on the river far below. Finally, dwell for just a moment on thoughts about yourself and the role you play on this earth. If you don't come away from such an interlude with a better understanding of nature and yourself, you will miss a large part of the precious gift your national parks preserve for you.

A fleecy blanket of fog from the valley of the Little Colorado River flows over Grand Canyon's rim and dissipates as it meets warm air rising from the canyon floor. PHOTO BY JIM TALLON

Back cover: Toroweap in the western portion of Grand Canyon overlooks wilderness solitude and an unparalleled panorama of the Colorado River 3,000 feet below. PHOTO BY DAVID MUENCH

Books in this series: Grand Canyon, Zion, Canyon de Chelly, Yosemite, Dinosaur, Capitol Reef, Death Valley, Theodore Roosevelt, Shenandoah, Virgin Islands, Hawaii Volcanoes, Mount Rushmore, Petrified Forest, Yellowstone, Grand Teton, Haleakala, Mount McKinley

Printed by W. A. Krueger Co.
Separations by Color Masters